WS

Cooking a Meal

Rupert Matthews

FRANKLIN WATTS

NEW YORK • LONDON • SYDNEY

First published in 1999 by
Franklin Watts
96 Leonard Street
London
EC2A 4XD

Franklin Watts Australia
14 Mars Road
Lane Cove
NSW 2066
Australia

© Franklin Watts 1999

ISBN: 0 7496 3387 5 (hbk)
        0 7496 3586 X (pbk)
Dewey Decimal Classification 641.509
A CIP catalogue record for this book is available from the
British Library

Printed in Malaysia

Planning and production by Discovery Books Limited
Editors: Paul Humphrey, Claire Berridge
Design: Ian Winton
Art Director: Robert Walster
Illustrators: Stefan Chabluk, Mike White, Joanna Williams

Photographs:
4 Jeffrey L. Rotman/Corbis, 5 & 6 R. Sheridan/Ancient
Art & Architecture Collection, 7 British Museum/Werner
Forman Archive, 8 Pompeii Museum/Werner Forman
Archive, 9, 10 & 11 Mary Evans Picture Library, 12 R.
Sheridan/Ancient Art & Architecture Collection, 13 & 14
Mary Evans Picture Library, 15 top Robert Opie Collection,
15 bottom Andreas von Einsiedel/National Trust
Photographic Library, 17, 18 & 19 top Mary Evans Picture
Library, 19 bottom Robert Opie Collection, 21 top Corbis-
Bettman, 21 bottom Gary W. Carter/Corbis, 22 top Robert
Opie Collection, 23 bottom Mary Evans Picture Library,
24 top and 25 Robert Opie Collection, 28 Charles E.
Rotkin/Corbis, 29 Last Resort Picture Library

Acknowledgements:
Discovery Books would like to thank the following
for the use of material: Burger King, Sun Valley,
Philips, Whirlpool

Contents

The mammoth hunters

Thousands of years ago people could not buy food in shops. When they were hungry they had to go hunting. Many people hunted mammoths. Mammoths were bigger than elephants. Hunters would eat them and live in homes made from mammoth bones and skins.

Today many people around the world still hunt for food.

Hunting and gathering

To catch a mammoth, hunters would trap one in a pit, then kill it with long spears. Tools made from a stone called flint were used to cut the meat into smaller pieces. These were then hung up to dry so that they could be stored and eaten many days later. People also gathered berries, roots and leaves from wild plants to eat.

Prehistoric cooking

People first used fire to cook food about 400,000 years ago. Meat which needed long, slow cooking was cooked in firepits. A large pit was lined with stones and then a fire built inside it. The meat was wrapped in animal skin or large leaves. When the fire died down, the food was put on the stones. Then the pit was covered with soil, which kept the heat inside for slow cooking.

These pots are from prehistoric France.

Stews of meat and wild plants were made in large leather bags. Stones were heated in the fire, then dropped into the bag to heat the liquid and food inside.

A prehistoric meal by the fire.

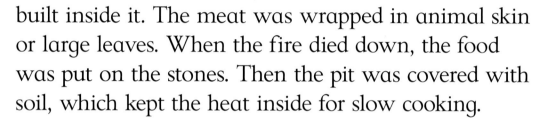

A Babylonian banquet

People began farming about 12,000 years ago. Instead of hunting wild animals and gathering plants, people grew crops and kept tame animals. This meant that new foods came into use. When people began living in cities, food preparation and types of food eaten changed again. There are tales of huge feasts taking place in the larger cities like Babylon.

This decorated bowl from Babylon is 6,000 years old.

The first ovens

Ovens were built of clay and enclosed the food in a steady heat. The heat from the fire could be made hot or smouldering, so food could be roasted quickly or baked slowly. Pottery made new types of cooking possible. Soups could be kept simmering in pots placed close to a fire. Pots were used as moulds for pastries, loaves and other foods.

Daily bread

The early farmers grew wheat and barley. The grains were ground into flour. This could then be added to soups to make them thick and nutritious, or used to make pastry and a type of flat bread like modern pitta bread.

This Assyrian slab from 1,000BC shows the different stages in food preparation.

A typical meal

A typical meal in Babylon might begin with lettuce and cucumber salad, followed by a stew of lamb, onions and prunes. Cherries and apples were often eaten raw, or made into a chilled dessert. Poor people ate less meat and more porridge than rich people.

A Babylonian feast.

Classical feasts

Classical Greece and Rome lasted from about 400BC to AD400. At first the cooking in this period was simple: roast meat served with bread, olives and wine. Later, increasing wealth meant that people spent more time and money on meals to impress their friends. The oldest known cookbook was written by Marcus Gabius Apicius, a rich nobleman who lived in Rome in about AD20. The Romans called small cakes *apicia* in his honour.

The two conical stones in this Roman bakery from 100BC were the mills for grinding wheat into flour.

In the kitchen

A typical kitchen had a clay oven for baking and a pit of charcoal for frying and boiling. The Greeks and Romans had metal pots and pans, and used metal grids to suspend food over a fire, like a barbecue. Rich families had slaves to do the cooking for them.

Dinner games

The main meal of the day was in the evening. Dinner guests ate with their fingers while lying on a couch. At the end of the meal, Greek men played a game called cottabos. A target was chosen and small amounts of wine were flicked at it from cups.

All Roman towns had taberna, or taverns. Workers could stop for wine and a snack of bread with olive oil or cheese.

This ancient Greek painting shows a banquet scene.

Imperial feasts

The Roman emperors were famous for lavish meals. They feasted on fried tongues of larks, dormice stuffed with herbs and whole roast ostrich. People would eat a full meal, then go outside and make themselves sick so that they had room for more food.

In the Middle Ages

After the fall of the Roman Empire travelling became unsafe and cooks were unable to import exotic foods such as ostriches or eastern spices. Instead, people used whatever foods they could find locally.

Fire masters

One of the most important jobs in cooking a medieval meal was tending the fire. Roasting meats needed a 'bright fire', a very hot fire glowing red or yellow. Stews needed a 'grey fire', when the flames had died down but the embers were still hot.

In large kitchens a young boy would be trained to provide the right type of fire for the cook.

There are no forks on the table because in the 1400s they hadn't been invented yet!

Stopping the rot

A major problem was keeping food fresh. Food produced in the summer had to be preserved for use in the winter. Fruits were often dried, and vegetables were pickled in vinegar.

This medieval picture shows all the stages in preserving meat.

Salting and smoking

It was expensive to feed animals in the winter, so most were slaughtered in the autumn. The meat was then dried, salted or smoked to stop it rotting. Bacon made from salted and smoked pork was very popular. Any meat which did start to go off was cooked with strong spices to mask the rank taste.

Medieval gingerbread

1 Mix 500g (1 lb) warm honey with 500g (1 lb) breadcrumbs, 2 tsp of cinnamon, 2 tsp of ground ginger and 1 tsp of pepper.

2 Line a shallow cake tin with some grease-proof paper or foil and pour the mixture in.

3 Place in refrigerator for two hours, then turn out and cut into squares.

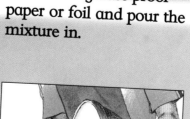

Discovering new foods

Many food crops have been grown in one place, and then exported or transplanted to another area as they have become popular. Some of our most familiar ingredients have their origins thousands of kilometres away.

Sugar and spice

During the Middle Ages, only food which could stay fresh could be transported over long distances. By about 1300 spices from Malaya, India and southern China were being transported to Europe. These spices included cloves, mace,

Merchants trading food and spices.

saffron, ginger, cinnamon, cardamom and pepper. Sugar was exported from Syria and several islands in the Mediterranean.

Food from the New World

Many food plants come from South America. Potatoes, tomatoes, peppers, chillies and aubergines only reached Europe when Europeans discovered that America existed. In northern Europe potatoes became so popular they took the place of bread.

Spaghetti from China

In 1295 Marco Polo returned to Italy after spending time in China. He is said to have brought back the idea of mixing flour and eggs to make pasta. Until then, nobody in Italy had eaten spaghetti.

▲ A fifteenth-century illustration of Marco Polo.

Chocolate

Chocolate was the royal food of the Mexican Aztecs. It was made into a hot drink with water, honey and eggs. Chocolate was also chopped up with chillies and eaten with roast turkey.

Tea and coffee

Coffee grows wild in Sudan in Africa and by 1540 a drink made from dried coffee beans had been developed in Turkey. The drink was very expensive, but had spread across Europe by about 1650. Tea originated in China and was first brought to Europe in the late 1500s. Most tea is now grown in India or Africa.

Home on the range

In the early 1800s, technology solved problems which had bothered cooks for centuries. The cheap, mass-produced iron of the industrial revolution was used to make 'kitcheners' or 'cooking ranges' and to fashion a wide variety of inexpensive new tools.

A maid-servant in a kitchen of the late nineteenth century.

The open range

The simplest ranges consisted of a metal fireplace over which were metal grids for grilling and roasting. On one side of the fire was a metal oven heated by the fire. On the other side was a water tank which produced hot water. Over this was a metal plate hot enough to simmer stews.

Kitcheners

Middle-class families now had a kitchener for cooking. These ingenious iron objects used the heat from a single fire for many tasks. The coal fire was enclosed in an iron case. Immediately above the fire was a hot plate for frying or quick boiling. Next to the fire was a hot oven for baking, and above it was another hot plate. There was also a cool oven for slow cooking. A rack kept plates warm and a water jacket produced hot water.

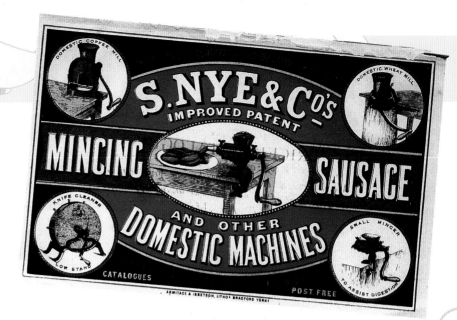

An advertisement for kitchen equipment in the 1890s.

Pots and pans

Cheap iron was also used to produce pots and pans. The average cook no longer had to make do with one pan for all jobs. A set of weight scales meant that cooks could at last measure ingredients accurately.

A selection of nineteenth-century kitchen spoons.

Society dinners

Cooking a meal for a wealthy family in the nineteenth century was a major task. Several servants would work hard for hours beforehand to produce a magnificent meal which was perfectly presented. A typical dinner for 18 people might consist of five courses.

In the kitchen

Cooking the meal involved getting each dish ready at the correct time. Cook was in charge in the kitchen. During the day she would buy the ingredients for dinner and have them delivered.

Behind the scenes of a Victorian banquet.

Meanwhile the kitchen-maid cleaned the kitchen and larder and the scullery-maid laid out any pots, pans and tools the cook would need. The cook and kitchen-maids would begin cooking about six hours before dinner was due to be served. After dinner the servants would sit down to eat the left-overs.

Serving dinner

The butler was in charge of serving dinner. He made certain that all the silver, cutlery and plates were in their proper place on the table. Then he called the guests to dinner.

The butler stood behind the host during dinner. He served the wine and made certain that the other staff served dishes properly. At least one footman helped the butler.

Mrs Beeton

In 1861 Mrs Beeton of Epsom, in Surrey, published *A Book of Household Management*. It was so popular that it was reprinted many times, and is still available today. Mrs Beeton went on to write other popular cookery books.

The bread line

In the nineteenth century poor people had little choice of what to eat. The basic food for those who could not afford even bread was gruel. Barley or oats were boiled in water until they became a thick soup. The gruel might be flavoured with egg, butter, beef fat or goose grease to make it more appetising.

Finding meat

In country areas men might go poaching, catching animals on land that did not belong to them. Many landowners allowed the local poor to poach rabbits and pigeons, so long as they did not hunt the more valuable pheasants and hares.

A simple family meal in the late nineteenth century.

Pigs and chickens could be kept in small areas, such as a backyard. Many families would keep a few chickens to provide eggs, while several families might join together to keep a pig.

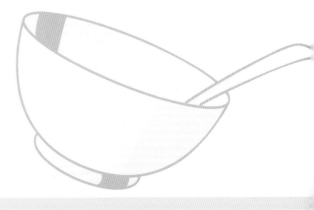

Preserved foods became popular in the late nineteenth century.

Tinned meat

During the 1860s tinned foods became available. Sheep in Australia and cattle in the American West could be raised cheaply, then the meat was tinned and shipped to cities.

Gas cookers

It was too expensive for poor families to build a fire to cook each meal in the summer. In 1884 gas companies started renting out cookers to encourage people to use gas. This meant poor people could switch on a burner, cook their meal and switch it off without wasting energy.

A gas cooker from 1910.

Frontier cooking

As settlers moved out on to the open prairies of North America they found that many familiar crops would not grow out West. Other foods were found in plenty, but were unknown back East. The westerners developed a new style of unfussy cooking which has now become popular.

Johnny Appleseed

In 1801 John Chapman of Boston headed west, taking with him a load of apple seeds. Before his death in 1847, Chapman planted thousands of apple trees for pioneer farmers and became known as Johnny Appleseed. Apple pie became a favourite dessert in American cooking.

In later life, Johnny Appleseed was famous for wearing his cooking pot on his head.

Chuck wagon

When cowboys were driving their cattle to sell at the railroad, they had to take all their food with them. This meant they could only have food which would not spoil on the hot journey. Dried beans, bacon, molasses and flour all kept well. So most days cowboys ate boiled beans and bacon with flour tortillas, with sweet pancakes as a treat.

Buffalo hunters cook over a fire in the American West.

An American settler's kitchen in 1850.

Frontier families

The first farmers to arrive on the western plains were given 64 hectares (160 acres) of land. They grew wheat, corn, pumpkins and various vegetables, while chickens and pigs were kept with, perhaps, a small dairy herd. Providing a meal often meant cooking food that could be put out for the family to help themselves to as they came home from work in the fields.

At the flick of a switch

From the 1880s onwards electricity became increasingly common in homes. Electric appliances were invented to make cooking easier. Soon many people would think that cooking a meal without electricity was almost impossible.

Electric ovens

The first electric ovens were manufactured by Carpenter Electric in Minnesota in 1891. However, electricity was more expensive than gas, and electric rings could not be made waterproof if a saucepan boiled over. These problems were not solved until the 1930s, after which sales boomed. By the 1950s there were as many electric cookers as gas ovens.

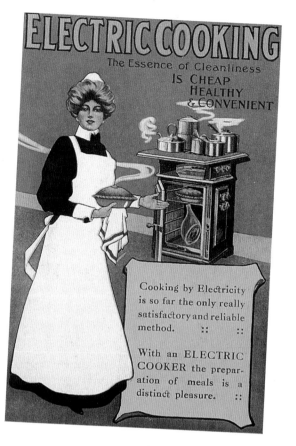

An early advertisement for electric cookers.

Food processors

In the 1950s British inventor Ken Wood produced a small electric chopping machine. Today most kitchens have electric food processors, mixers and blenders. Instead of spending time slicing vegetables or mixing dough, the modern cook can just flick a switch.

Refrigeration

Large industrial refrigeration plants had been invented in the 1850s, but a small fridge was not invented until 1913. At first fridges were used by stores to keep foods fresh. In 1930 Clarence Birdseye began producing frozen foods so that shops could offer vegetables, such as peas and spinach, out of season.

Before refrigeration, an ice chest was an old-fashioned way to keep food cold.

Are you safeguarding the health of your family with FRIGIDAIRE? It is an essential to modern housekeeping!

Home fridges did not become common until the 1950s when a cheap manufacturing process was invented. They changed domestic life at once. Instead of shopping every day for that day's meals, people could buy food once a week.

A 1920s advertisement for refrigerators.

In times of war

During a war, governments may limit, or ration, the amount of food that people can buy. This means ships can import weapons instead of food and people in the armed forces get enough to eat. In World War II, nearly every nation introduced rationing. People were given vouchers which they gave to shopkeepers every time they bought food. If they did not have a voucher they were not allowed to buy food.

This was one week's ration in wartime.

A wartime cookbook.

Ersatz

When some foods are difficult to buy, people use substitutes, or 'ersatz' foods, instead. Coffee can be made to go further by adding chicory or even roasted acorns. Margarine made from vegetable oils and fats was introduced as a cheap alternative to butter.

24

Making do

Chicken and fresh eggs soon became scarce in Britain after war broke out. Powdered eggs from America were imported instead, but tasted so unpleasant that they were soon

restricted to use in baking. At the same time, most countries with rationing had special foods for children. Milk, eggs and cheese were given to children to help them grow properly.

Wartime 'ersatz' foods.

Close to home

Foods produced in a country were rarely rationed. In the USA, bread and flour were not rationed, but they were in Britain. In India, tea was not rationed at all, but in Britain each person was allowed only 50g (2oz) per week and in Germany it could not be bought at all.

Government posters encouraged people to watch what they bought.

MINISTRY of FOOD

Let your SHOPPING help our SHIPPING

PLAN YOUR MEALS TO AVOID WASTE

Modern convenience

Convenience foods and takeaways have become increasingly popular in recent years. People either do not have the time to cook or they cannot be bothered. Some of these meals have been criticised for not being very healthy. They may contain large quantities of fat, and few fresh vegetables or fruits. These meals also need to be carefully handled to avoid problems with hygiene.

The king of convenience foods, the hamburger is an international success.

Fast food chains promise that meals bought anywhere in the world will be the same.

Popular foods

Hamburgers and pizzas were invented in Europe, and became popular once they were adopted in the United States. In Britain, fish fried in batter and served with chips has been a popular takeaway food for many years. Most towns have at least one fish and chip shop.

Prepared meals

Many shops now sell complete meals which are fully cooked and need only to be warmed up at home. These meals are produced in large factories where thousands of dishes are prepared at a time. They are packed in plastic to keep them fresh and chilled, ready for transport to the shops.

Ready meals being prepared in a factory.

Microwaves

Food in a microwave oven is bombarded with high frequency radio waves. These collide with water molecules in the food, causing them to vibrate and heat up. In this way food is cooked from the inside outwards, unlike other forms of cooking. Microwave ovens can heat food quickly and efficiently, and are especially good at heating prepared meals or left-overs.

A microwave oven.

27

The global kitchen

In previous periods, people ate whatever foods grew near to where they lived. It was difficult to move food long distances because either it went rotten or people would not pay the high price of transport. However, since the mid-nineteenth century foods have been moved long distances.

A little bit of China in New York.

Greater variety

People from many different cultures have moved around the world, and have brought their ways of cooking food with them. In many countries different cultures have lent ingredients and cooking styles. Chinese restaurants are found around the world, as are Greek, Italian, Korean and German to name a few.

Mixing cultures

During the past 50 years, many people from the old British Empire in India have moved to live in Britain. Since then, Indian curries and tandoori baked foods have become some of the most popular cuisines in Britain. Today we can cook a meal which has ingredients from many different countries. We enjoy a wider variety of tastes than our ancestors and spend less time actually cooking than ever before.

Indian cuisine is now the most popular restaurant food in Britain.

Check the countries

1 Gather a selection of tins and food packaging from your kitchen cupboards.

2 Write down the country of origin of each item.

3 Find those countries on a map. Which food has come the farthest? Was it the most expensive?

Timeline

BC

c 400,000	First use of fire for cooking by humans.
c 50,000	Humans live by hunting mammoths and other large animals, and by collecting wild plants.
c 10,000	Humans start to farm by growing crops and keeping animals.
c 8,000	Pottery vessels are used to stew foods and soups.
c 6,000	The first ovens are built.
c 800	First iron cooking pots are made.

AD

20	Marcus Gabius Apicius becomes famous in Rome for inventing new recipes and discovering exotic types of food.
410	The fall of the Roman Empire makes travelling unsafe, so people use whatever foods can be found locally.
1295	Italian Marco Polo returns from China with the recipe for pasta.
1380	William Taillevent, cook to the King of France, writes the cookbook *Le Viandier*.
1492	Christopher Columbus reaches the Americas. New foods, including potatoes, tomatoes, chocolate and turkey are taken from the Americas to Europe.
c 1540	Coffee begins to be made into a drink in Turkey.
c 1575	Tea is exported from China to Europe and other parts of the world.
c 1770	The Industrial Revolution begins in Britain. New ways of making iron make the metal cheap enough for ordinary people to buy pots and pans for cooking in different ways.
1801	Birth of John Chapman, who planted apple orchards across America.
1830	Kitchen ranges are introduced.
1861	English journalist Mrs Isabella Beeton first publishes her *Book of Household Management*, which includes recipes and information about different types of food. Updated for modern times, it is still available today.
1860s	Tinned food becomes widely available, allowing meat to be exported from Australia and the American West to feed poor people in cities.
1884	Gas companies start renting out cookers to encourage people to use gas.
1891	The first electric oven is invented.
1913	Domestic fridges are invented and put on sale.
1939	World War II begins. Food rationing is introduced in most countries involved in the war.
1947	First microwave ovens manufactured in Massachusetts, USA.

Glossary

Assyria A country north of ancient Babylon.

Aztec A people who lived in what is now Mexico.

Babylon A large and wealthy city which stood in Iraq.

Charcoal A virtually smokeless fuel burnt in barbecues and some types of oven.

Ersatz A type of food which imitates another.

Firepit A hole in the ground filled with stones which were heated by a wood fire. Food was then cooked on the stones.

Gruel A type of soup thickened by flour or oats.

Mammoth A type of hairy elephant which once lived in northern Europe and Asia, but which no longer exists.

Mutton The meat from an adult sheep.

Poaching Hunting animals without the permission of the land owner.

Porridge A food made by soaking crushed grains in water or milk, then boiling the mixture until it is thick.

Range Cooking equipment which includes an oven, hot plate and other features, all heated by a single fire.

Rationing A system of controlling the amount of food people are allowed to buy, especially in times of war.

Squatter A person who occupies buildings or land, often illegally.

Further reading

Berriedale-Johnson, Michelle, *The British Museum Cookbook*, British Museum Publications, 1995

Millard, Anne, *Everyday Life: Ancient Egypt, Ancient Greece, Ancient Rome*, Usborne Publishing Ltd, 1997

Robins, Deri, *The Kids' Round the World Cookbook*, Kingfisher Books, 1994

Index